G Crawford
Sedona, Arizona
2023

THE MAGIC IN THE MUD

STORY AND ILLUSTRATIONS
BY
GERALD CRAWFORD

FIRST EDITION

ISBN 0-9672996-0-8

The Magic in the Mud / by Gerald Crawford
illustrated by Gerald Crawford -1st ed.

Summary: A boy who looks at the world differently
discovers the magic of creating, finding the magic
of art where others just see dirt.

[1. books about art, / creativity, 2. mud, 3. earth, / nature, / magic,
4. architecture, 5. southwest, 6. fiction, 7. Sedona, Arizona,]

USE A MIRROR OR USE YOUR MIND
TO READ
THIS SPECIAL MESSAGE!

ART IS WHERE YOU MAKE IT HAPPEN!

TO MY FAMILY AND TO
ALL WHO HAVE FELT THE MAGIC.

It was spring in the little village,
nestled below the towering sandstone cliffs,
when he first discovered it.

Living in this special place,
the boy had everything he needed.
He had his family and friends, he had the creek
and the woods, and he had the magic.

It was in the not so distant past that spring,
following days of rain, when he found
the soft red dirt could turn into the most wonderful,
magical, sticky red mud!

Sometimes, he did look at things differently.

Most of the village would agree that this was
indeed a special place. The red cliffs surrounding
them were often called a magnificent wonder of nature!

5

EXCEPT AS A NUISANCE,
FEW SAID MUCH OF THE SOFT RED MUD.

IT STAINED THEIR SOCKS AND STUCK TO THEIR SHOES.

IT TURNED THE RAIN WATER RED
AND WAS ALWAYS GETTING INTO THE HOUSE!

8

NEAR THE BOY'S HOUSE, BY ONE OF THE MANY TRAILS
THAT LED DOWN TO THE CREEK, WAS A BIG PILE OF RED DIRT.

LIKE THE DIRT AROUND THE VILLAGE, NO ONE PAID MUCH
ATTENTION TO ONE PILE OF WET RED DIRT.

SEEING THINGS DIFFERENTLY,
THE BOY DID NOTICE IT.

HE FOUND IT SLIPPING INTO HIS THOUGHTS
MORE AND MORE AS HE BEGAN TO SENSE SOMETHING
UNUSUAL ABOUT THE BIG PILE OF SOFT, WET, DIRT!

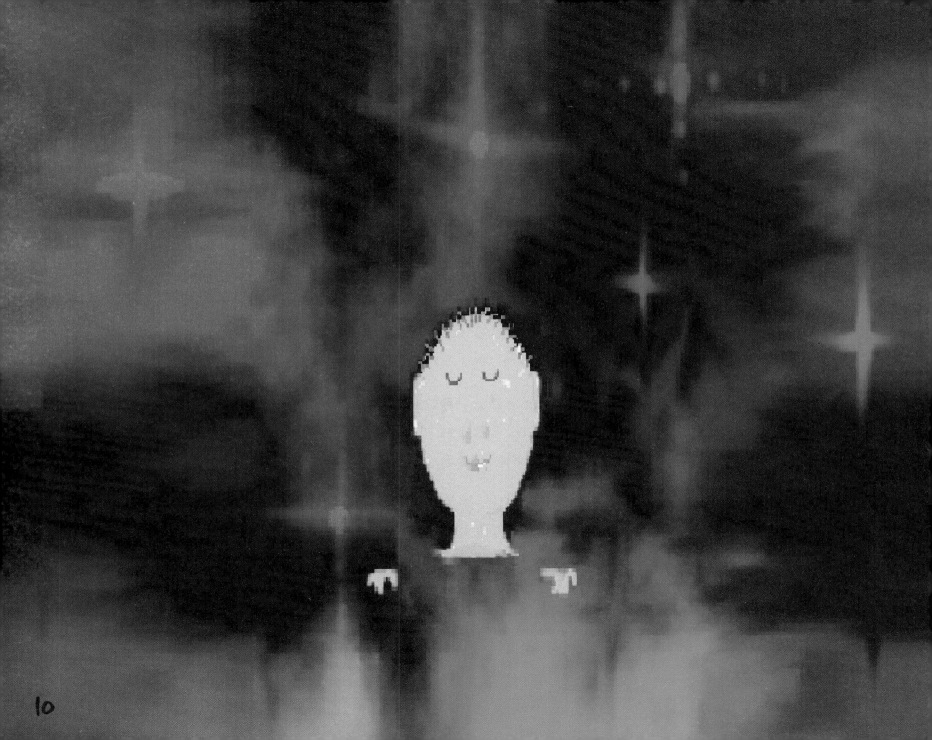

10

AS THE BOY WAS FALLING ASLEEP THAT NIGHT WITH
IDEAS FLYING INTO HIS MIND LIKE SPARKS
OFF HIS DAD'S GRINDER,
HE SAW WHAT THAT PILE OF DIRT MIGHT BE.
WHAT HE SAW MADE HIM VERY HAPPY!

12

AS HE HEADED OUT THE NEXT DAY TOWARDS THE PILE OF RED DIRT,
THE AIR WAS FILLED WITH A SENSE OF SPRING.
HE WAS REMINDED OF THE STRONG FRAGRANT YELLOW BARBERRY,
THE SWEET AROMA OF THE PINK MANZANITA, AND THE BUZZ OF
ACTIVITY SURROUNDING THE COLORFUL
TREES OF THE VILLAGE ORCHARDS.
WITH QUICK, CAREFULLY PLACED STEPS, AVOIDING
THE FRESH SHOOTS OF THE DELICATE WILD ONIONS,
HE TOOK THE SHORTEST
ROUTE TO THE BIG PILE OF RED DIRT.
THERE IT STOOD,
WIDE AND WET BEFORE A FRESH, GHOSTLY
GREEN BANK OF DESERT SALTBUSH.

As the boy climbed the pile, a special kind of feeling
began to surround him.

He reached down, took a handful of the soft
red mud, and started working it between his hands.
The feeling of the earth in his hands and the
glow of the warm sun felt as comforting as
squeezing in close between his mother and father
on the soft sofa of their warm, safe home.

With the vision in his mind as fresh
as the spring blossoms, he began to build.

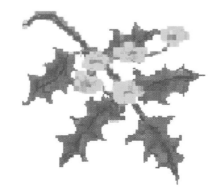

He found that the cool earth,
soft from the winter's freeze,
was easily dug and piled.
As the pile grew, he noticed his ideas changing.
Shapes in the pile seemed to suggest the next shape,
that would suggest the next, and the next,
and the next!
It was as if the mud
were making suggestions to him!

17

18

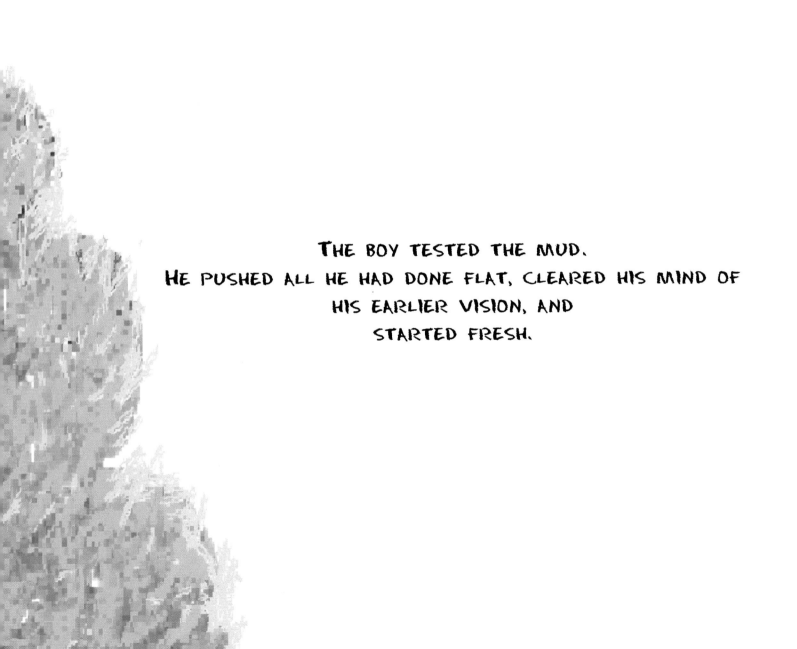

THE BOY TESTED THE MUD.
HE PUSHED ALL HE HAD DONE FLAT, CLEARED HIS MIND OF
HIS EARLIER VISION, AND
STARTED FRESH.

20

As he took the cool wet mud into his hands,
the warm comforting feeling came over him again.
New ideas entered his mind as he felt a
magic that seemed to come from the
earth itself!

THE MAGIC STAYED WITH HIM
AS HE DUG AND PRESSED
AND PATTED THE PLIABLE EARTH INTO EACH
NEW SHAPE.

AS THE BOY WORKED, THE MAGIC BECAME STRONGER, AND
IDEAS SEEMED CLEARER.

AT THE TOP OF THE PILE
HE BUILT FOUR WALLS. HE FORMED A DOORWAY THROUGH
ONE, USING THE BLOCKS THAT HE HAD SQUEEZED
INTO SHAPE WITH HIS HANDS.
CAREFULLY HE PRESSED THE
EDGES SMOOTH.

23

FOR A ROOF, HE THOUGHT OF THE INDIAN CLIFF DWELLINGS HIDDEN BELOW THE TOWERING RED SANDSTONE CLIFFS. THEY ONCE HAD ROOFS OF LOGS, STICKS AND GRASS, COVERED WITH THE SAME MAGICAL MUD, AND HE WONDERED IF THEY, TOO, HAD FELT THE MAGIC IN THE MUD...

HE COLLECTED SMALL TWIGS, CAREFULLY LAYING THEM SIDE BY SIDE TO FORM THE CEILING. FINALLY, HE GENTLY COVERED THEM WITH THE SOFT WET MUD.

HE FOUND A SMALL BLOCK OF WOOD, THAT WHEN PRESSED
INTO THE SOFT MUD, STEP BY STEP, MADE
PERFECT STAIRS!
IT WORKED SO NICE HE DID IT TWICE!

28

HE MADE A SOLID MUD BUILDING BELOW
THE STEPS. THEN HE DISCOVERED THAT IF HE PRESSED THE END OF
THE BLOCK INTO THE MUD, IT MADE GREAT
WINDOWS AND DOORS! THE MUD SEEMED FULL OF MAGIC!

As the morning raced by,
he continued using the magic
as he built down and around
the big pile of red dirt.

32

THE MAGIC DREW HIM IN AS HE
CONCENTRATED
ON THE
MUD CONSTRUCTIONS.

SO MUCH SO THAT WHEN HIS
FRIENDS CAME BY,
HEADED TO THE CREEK
TO SKIP SOME STONES,
HE COULD HARDLY
LOOK UP,
HE COULD NOT LEAVE
THE MAGIC IN THE MUD...

34

WHEN IT WAS LATER THAN HE SHOULD HAVE STAYED, HE
LOOKED ON WHAT HE HAD DONE AND FELT VERY HAPPY!

35

36

THE BOY WAS SO PLEASED
WITH HIS CREATIONS
THAT HE SPENT
THE WHOLE EVENING WITH
HIS HEAD IN THE CLOUDS.

HE WAS SO EXCITED,
AND HIS MIND
SO FILLED WITH IDEAS,
THAT HE DIDN'T THINK OF THE MAGIC
UNTIL HIS HEAD TOUCHED HIS PILLOW!

HOW COULD HE HAVE FORGOTTEN THE
MAGIC?

HE WORRIED. WOULD THE MAGIC
STILL BE IN THE MUD TOMORROW?

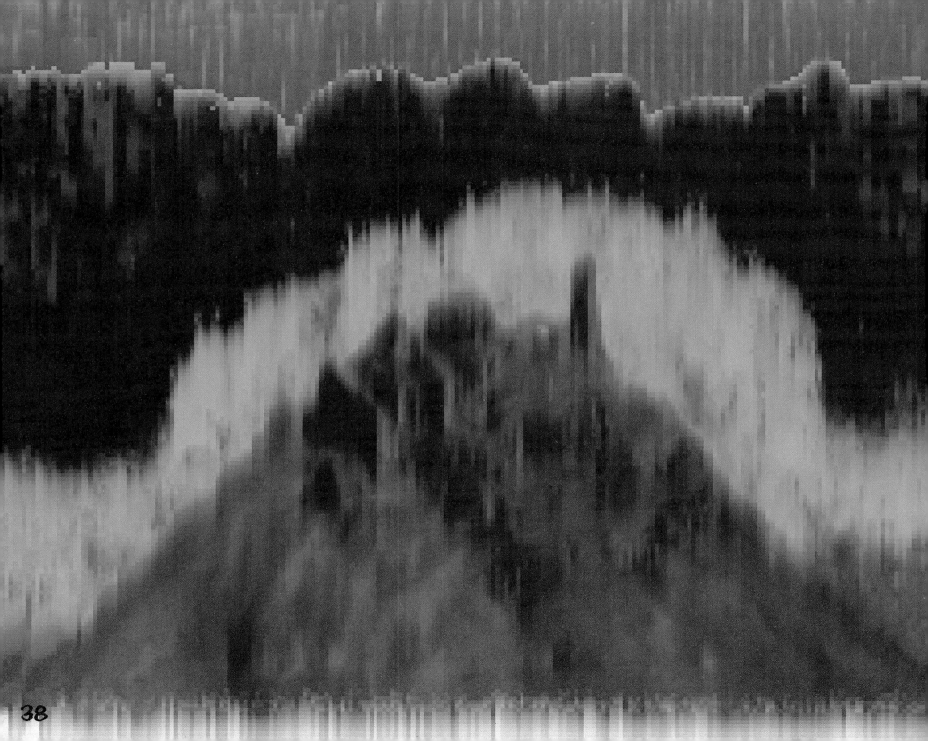

38

It was hard to get to sleep!
Rain!
His dad had said during dinner
that it might start sometime in the night.
He could hardly hear it at first.
Rain.
Harder and harder it sounded on his roof, as it
dripped from the eaves!
The sounds made for an anxious night,
but in his visions of tumbling earthen walls,
was the gift of more mud.
He thought of what could be made,
and what he saw seemed
quite wonderful!

39

40

He was back at the big pile of dirt the
next day, and much to his surprise
his creations had weathered the
night's storm!
They were soft and wet with their edges
rounded, but they were still standing.

42

THE NIGHT'S STORM STILL THREATENED AS THE BOY BEGAN
TO WORK THE COLD WET EARTH. JUST THEN HE REALIZED
HOW SOONER OR LATER THE RAIN OR SNOW OR A KID WOULD
DESTROY ALL HE HAD MADE..
HE KNEW THE POWER OF BOTH KIDS AND EROSION.
HE KNEW THAT THE POWER OF THE STORMS HAD SHAPED THE
RED STONE CLIFFS. HE HAD SEEN THE WINTER'S FREEZE TURN THE
RED DIRT FROM ROCK HARD TO A SOFT-TEXTURED FLUFF THAT
COULD TURN TO DUST IN ONLY A MATTER OF DAYS.

WHY, HE THOUGHT, SHOULD HE SPEND ANOTHER DAY ON SOMETHING
THAT COULD NEVER LAST? MAYBE THE VILLAGE WAS RIGHT, AND THE OLD
RED DIRT WAS JUST A NUISANCE.

HE LOOKED AT HIS COLD HANDS, COVERED WITH THE SOFT RED MUD.
THEN HE REACHED DOWN AND TOOK ANOTHER HANDFUL.
AS HE WORKED THE WET MUD, HE STARTED AGAIN
TO FEEL THE WARM COMFORTING FEELING. HE STARTED
TO SEE THE VISIONS OF THINGS HE COULD BUILD, AND
AGAIN, HE FELT THE POWER OF
THE MAGIC IN THE MUD!

44

SO THE BOY STAYED,
AND WITH THE
MAGIC, HIS
BUILDING CONTINUED....

45

GAMBLE'S QUAIL

LILY

SKIPPING STONE

WHITETAIL DEER

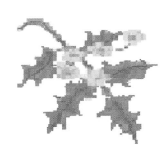

MANZANITA

BARBERRY

COYOTE

SALTBUSH

WILD ONION

COTTONTAIL RABBIT

OAK CREEK

46

About the Author
and the Book

Gerald Crawford, an Arizona native, is a self-taught artist, who for more than thirty years has explored the magic of creating. He has created works for museums, historical societies, private collectors, the President, and now for children his first book. The mud is real, the magic is real. You might want to look in your own backyard, the magic of creating may be closer than you think. Gerald and Linda live in Arizona with their two sons, in a home they built themselves out of the magical
RED MUD!

ART IS WHERE <u>YOU</u> MAKE IT HAPPEN!

RED MUD PRESS WOULD LIKE TO ENCOURAGE ALL
PARENTS TO HELP THEIR CHILDREN FIND THEIR OWN PERSONAL MAGIC,
READ TO THEM, AND BE KIND TO THIS VERY SPECIAL PLACE WE CALL EARTH.